Spanish Missions

JOHN PERRITANO

Children's Press®
An Imprint of Scholastic Inc.
New York Toronto London Auckland Sydney
Mexico City New Delhi Hong Kong
Danbury, Connecticut

Content Consultant

Kristina W. Foss

Museum Director, Santa Barbara Mission Museum

Library of Congress Cataloging-in-Publication Data

Perritano, John.
 Spanish missions / by John Perritano.
     p. cm.—(A true book)
 Includes bibliographical references and index.
 ISBN-13: 978-0-531-20575-4 (lib. bdg.)   978-0-531-21238-7 (pbk.)
 ISBN-10: 0-531-20575-4 (lib. bdg.)   0-531-21238-6 (pbk.)

 1. Missions, Spanish—Southwest, New—History—Juvenile literature. 2.
Spaniards—Southwest, New—History—Juvenile literature. 3. Indians of
North America—Missions—Southwest, New—History—Juvenile literature.
4. Franciscans—Missions—Southwest, New—History—Juvenile literature.
5. Southwest, New—History—To 1848—Juvenile literature. I. Title.
II. Series.

 HE6375.P65.P476 2010
 266'.279—dc22   2009017742

All rights reserved. Published in 2010 by Children's Press, an imprint of Scholastic Inc.
Published simultaneously in Canada. Printed in China.
SCHOLASTIC, CHILDREN'S PRESS, A TRUE BOOK, and associated logos are trademarks and/or registered trademarks of Scholastic Inc.

1 2 3 4 5 6 7 8 9 10 R 19 18 17 16 15 14 13 12 11 10   62

Find the Truth!

Everything you are about to read is true *except* for one of the sentences on this page.

Which one is **TRUE**?

T or F All of the Spanish missions built in what is now the United States are in ruins.

T or F Native Americans lived at the Spanish missions.

Find the answers in this book.

Bell from Mission San Luis Obispo de Tolosa in San Luis Obispo, California

Contents

THE **BIG** TRUTH!

Mission Life

**Native Americans work
on mission farmland.**

4

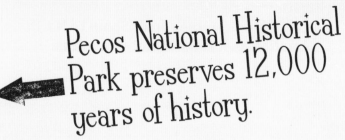

Pecos National Historical Park preserves 12,000 years of history.

Mission San Juan Capistrano in San Antonio, Texas

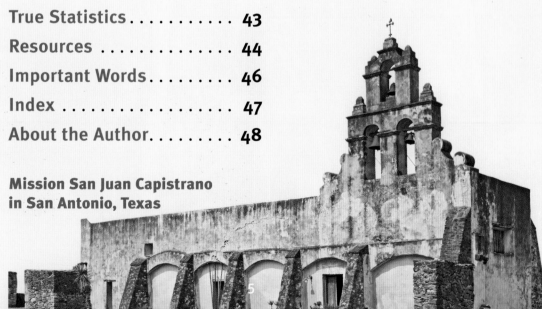

Columbus's journey from Spain to North America took more than two months.

CHAPTER 1

A New World

In 1492, explorer Christopher Columbus sailed west from Spain in search of a shorter water route to the **continent** of Asia. But instead of finding Asia, Columbus accidentally landed in North America. He reported back to the Spanish king and queen about the land he had found. The Spanish wanted to explore this new land for valuable gold, silver, and other minerals. They also wanted to use the land to grow crops for Spanish people who would come in search of these riches.

The first land Columbus reached in North America was in the Bahamas.

Starting Missions

In the early 1500s, Spain **claimed** much of North and South America as its own. Spain named what is now Mexico and the land farther north "New Spain."

In an effort to establish control over this new region and the Native people who lived there, Spain built villages known as missions. Spain sent soldiers and priests to do this work for them. Once they arrived, the priests tried to **convert** Native people to Christianity. The Spanish did not care that Native Americans already had their own religious beliefs.

Spanish soldiers raise a cross at a site where they will build a mission.

Presidios were built along the Florida coast to protect Spanish land from attacks by pirates and French and British troops.

Castillo de San Marcos is a presidio in St. Augustine, Florida.

Competing for Control

In 1565, the Spanish built their first mission in what is now the United States in St. Augustine, Florida. They continued building many other missions in the rest of Florida and in Georgia, North Carolina, and South Carolina. At the time, France and Great Britain also hoped to control land in North America. Spain built **presidios** (prih-SEE-dee-ohz), or forts, near some missions to protect their land from French and British attacks.

The Spanish explored the Southwest searching for gold.

Gold!

After conquering and establishing control over Mexico, the Spanish set their sights on areas to the north. They had heard stories about cities north of Mexico that were full of gold and silver. In 1540, explorer Francisco Vázquez de Coronado (VAS-kes DEH kor-oh-NAH-doh) searched the American Southwest for gold. He found none. But in later years, Spanish explorers and priests followed in his footsteps. They founded missions in what are today Arizona, New Mexico, and Texas.

Soldiers for Spain

Spanish soldiers and explorers were known as **conquistadors** (kawn-KEES-tuh-dorz), or conquerors. They helped Spain expand its **empire** and spread Christianity to the Native people in North and South America. The conquistadors wore gleaming armor and rode horses brought from Spain, which people in these areas had never before seen. They also brought guns and swords, which the Native people did not have. With their powerful weapons, the conquistadors could easily establish control over the Native people.

A conquistador's helmet

Spanish conquistadors

CHAPTER 2

Taking Over the Southwest

In 1598, Juan de Oñate (WAN DEH oh-NYAH-tay), the governor of New Spain, led an **expedition** north from Mexico. King Philip II of Spain ordered Oñate to build missions, look for gold, and spread Christianity to Native peoples in the region. Oñate and 400 men, including 10 priests, traveled into the Rio Grande valley in what is now New Mexico. About 50,000 Native Americans lived here. Most belonged to a group of people known as the Pueblo.

Battle for Control

On their journey, Oñate's men demanded that the Pueblo people give them supplies and convert to Christianity. A group of Pueblo, called the Acoma, refused to give in to these demands. The Acoma rose up and killed at least 10 of Oñate's soldiers.

Oñate wanted revenge. He sent troops into the Acoma village. The troops killed many Acoma people and captured others. Oñate ordered that one foot of each male Acoma prisoner be cut off. He sentenced Acoma women and children to slavery.

Spanish soldiers took supplies from the Pueblo villages.

14

The End for Oñate

Many Spanish priests and settlers in New Mexico were shocked by Oñate's cruelty. They reported him to Spanish officials who were based in Mexico. The Spanish told Oñate that he was no longer governor. In 1614, they put him on trial and found him guilty. After his trial, Oñate was never allowed to return to New Mexico.

Juan de Oñate in New Mexico

Southwest Mission Life

With Oñate's entry into the American Southwest, the Spanish had claimed control over the region. From 1598 to 1756, they built more than 50 missions in what are today New Mexico and Arizona. The priests tried to make life at the missions the same as life in Spain. Some Native Americans lived at the missions, and the priests expected them to follow Spanish **customs**. But many Native people did not want to change the way they lived.

San Geronimo Church in the town of Taos (TOUS) is one of many churches the Spanish built in New Mexico.

The Pueblo Revolt

At the missions, Spanish priests and soldiers forced Native people to work for them for no pay. Over time, the Native people, especially the Pueblo, grew tired of this treatment.

In 1680, a Pueblo religious leader named Popé (poh-PAY) planned a **revolt**. Popé wanted the Pueblo people to free themselves of Spanish ways and Christianity. In the Pueblo Revolt, the Pueblo people defeated the Spanish and forced them out of New Mexico for 12 years.

Popé organized Native Americans from more than 70 villages to take part in the Pueblo Revolt.

Father Kino started San José de Tumacácori (ho-SAY DAY too-mah-KAH-kore-ee), the first mission in southern Arizona, in 1691.

Father Kino

As Spanish explorers and priests blazed trails in New Mexico, a priest named Eusebio Kino

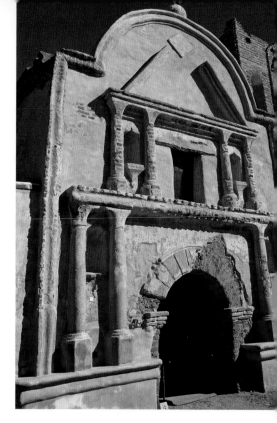

Mission San José de Tumacácori is located near Tucson (TOO-san), Arizona.

(yoo-SEB-yo KEE-no) built missions in a region called the Pimería Alta (pee-mare-EE-ah AL-tah). Today, this area includes northern Mexico and southern Arizona. Father Kino started more than 20 missions in the Pimería Alta. He spent 30 years traveling the region and made maps of the area.

Friend and Farmer

Unlike some priests sent by Spain, Father Kino was friendly toward the Native peoples in the Pimería Alta. He learned Native languages. He also tried to stop the Spanish from forcing Native Americans to do the dangerous work of digging for silver in mines.

Father Kino improved farming in the Pimería Alta. He built sheep and cattle ranches at missions and brought the first wheat, grapes, and olives to the region.

Father Kino studied the stars and was an expert in math.

The French claimed land in East Texas in 1682.

CHAPTER 3

Texas Missions

In the late 1600s, Spain and France were competing for control of what is now East Texas. By building missions, Spain was able to gain control of the area. Some Native people went to live at these missions. But by 1693, floods, **droughts** (DROWTS), and disease forced the East Texas missions to move to other areas.

The French settled in East Texas in 1685.

San Antonio Missions

Many of the East Texas missions moved west to an area along the San Antonio River. The first Spanish mission in the region, built in 1718, was Mission San Antonio de Valero. It is also known as the Alamo. Soon, Spain built four other missions along the San Antonio River. The river was important because it provided water for the missions' crops.

The Alamo is made of stone blocks that are 4 feet (1.2 meters) thick.

The Alamo

In 1821, Mexico became an independent country, no longer ruled by Spain. At the time, Mexico included the area that is now Texas. In 1835, some Texans rebelled against Mexican rule, using the Alamo as a fort. Mexican troops stormed the mission in 1836, killing hundreds of Texans. "Remember the Alamo" became the battle cry for the Texas soldiers. Texan troops eventually won a battle that allowed Texas to become independent from Mexico.

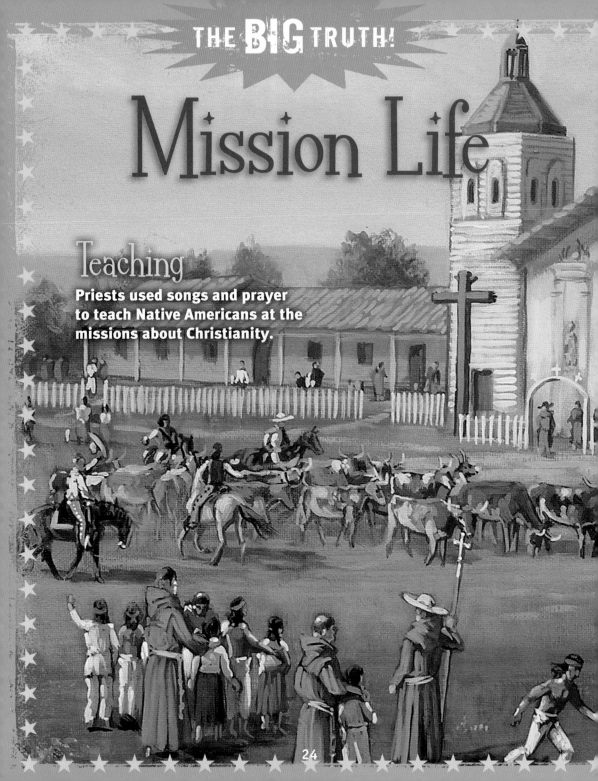

Mission Life

Teaching

Priests used songs and prayer to teach Native Americans at the missions about Christianity.

Both Native Americans and Spanish priests lived at the missions in North America. At most missions, Native people would work on the mission farms, construct buildings, cook, make items that people needed, and worship with the priests.

Daily Life

Native Americans planted and harvested crops to feed the people at the missions. Crops usually included corn, wheat, and beans.

Wheat was one of the most important mission crops.

CHAPTER 4

California Missions

Between 1769 and 1823, the Spanish built 21 missions along the California coast. The California missions were the most successful Spanish missions in what is now the United States. These missions' farms and ranches provided food for people throughout the region. Thousands of Native Americans moved to the missions and converted to Christianity.

More wheat was grown at Mission Santa Clara de Asís (ah-SEES) than at any other California mission.

The region of Baja lies to the south of what is now California.

Across Baja

In earlier years, the Spanish had tried to start missions in Baja, the land south of what is now the U.S. state of California. Father Kino started a mission in Baja, but a drought made it hard to grow food, and the mission lasted only two years. The Spanish thought Baja was an island. But during his travels, Father Kino discovered that Baja was actually connected to California. The Spanish would soon use Baja as a route to California.

Moving North

As the Spanish moved into northern California, they faced competition from Russia. Russian fur traders were active in this area, and the Spanish were worried that Russia would start settlements and claim the land. By once again building missions, the Spanish could establish their control over the region. A priest named Junípero Serra (hoo-NIP-eh-roh SEH-rah) was given the job of starting these missions in California.

Father Serra started nine missions in California.

The First California Mission

Four Spanish expeditions, which included both priests and soldiers, left Baja for California in 1769. Two expeditions traveled by boat, and two went overland. Father Serra and Gaspar de Portola (GAS-par DEH por-TOH-la), the governor of Baja, were part of one of these expeditions. They walked to southern California. In what is now San Diego, they built Mission San Diego, the first mission in California.

Father Serra explores the land where Mission San Diego would be built.

Spanish priests baptize a Native American child.

Life Changes

The California missions became home to many Native Americans. At the missions, the Spanish tried to convert them to Christianity. To convert Native people, priests would **baptize** them in a ceremony. About 17,000 Native Americans converted to Christianity during the first 60 years of the California missions. Many of them were also forced to work and live on the mission grounds.

Spanish soldiers oversee Native Americans at a presidio in San Francisco, California.

Learning to Live Together

Spanish priests and soldiers in California did not always agree about how to treat the Native people. The soldiers sometimes beat the Native people if they skipped prayers or work. This caused Native Americans to mistrust the Spanish, including the priests. The priests tried to keep the soldiers away from the Native Americans. Some Native Americans ran away from the missions, and others secretly practiced their own religions while living there.

Fighting Back

Some Native Americans fought back against the Spanish. In 1775, a group of Native people set fire to Mission San Diego. Its priests were not able to return to the mission for a year. In 1824, Native people revolted at Mission Santa Inés (ee-NAYS), north of the present-day city of Santa Barbara. The revolt spread to nearby missions and lasted more than a month before the Spanish regained control.

About 800 Native Americans attacked the San Diego mission.

The ruins of the Pecos Mission
stand near Santa Fe, New Mexico.

CHAPTER 5

The End of the Missions

By the late 1700s, the Spanish had abandoned missions in Texas and the Southwest for many reasons. The Spanish stopped taking care of some missions because they had run out of money. Attacks by Native people also drove the Spanish away. Diseases spread by Europeans killed many Native Americans. In some places, so many Native people died that the missions had no one left to work them, and they shut down.

When it was built, Pecos Mission was the largest Spanish structure in North America.

Missions Under Attack

By 1800, the Spanish missions were in trouble. Wars in Europe had caused Spain to pay less attention to its land in the Americas. Meanwhile, British

British troops attack Florida.

soldiers had destroyed many Spanish settlements and missions in eastern North America. Apache and Comanche people fought constantly with the Spanish in Texas and the Southwest.

Timeline of Spanish Missions

1565

Spain builds Mission Nombre de Dios (NOME-bray DEH DEE-oss), its first mission in what is now the United States, in St. Augustine, Florida.

1680

Popé leads the Pueblo Revolt, forcing the Spanish out of New Mexico.

Closing Missions

Once Mexico was no longer under Spain's rule, the country didn't have as much money. Its

The church of San José de Tumacácori, in Arizona, was abandoned in 1848.

government could not afford to give the missions in the Southwest what they needed to survive. In the 1820s and 1830s, the Mexican government closed the missions and divided up the land. Some priests and Native Americans tried to stay at the missions, but over time, they had to finally move away.

1718
The Spanish begin building missions along the San Antonio River in Texas.

1769
Father Serra starts the first California mission, in San Diego.

CHAPTER 6

Spanish Missions Today

Today, people can visit many Spanish missions in the southern and southwestern United States. Some have been rebuilt to look as they once did. Others were abandoned, and today they lie in ruins. Still others are national historic sites, protected by the U.S. government. Tourists can visit these sites to learn what life was like at the Spanish missions.

Nineteen of the California missions are still active churches.

Mission San Xavier del Bac is nicknamed "the White Dove of the Desert."

America's Oldest Missions

Some of the oldest Spanish missions in the United States are still churches. Mission Nombre de Dios in St. Augustine, Florida, was started in 1565, and there is still a church at the original site of this mission. Many people continue to worship at old mission churches in New Mexico and Arizona including Mission San Xavier del Bac (hav-EE-air DEL BAHK) in Tucson, Arizona.

Mission Trails

Missions in Texas and California attract many visitors. In San Antonio, Texas, five Spanish missions along the 8 miles (13 kilometers) of the Texas Mission Trail are open to visitors. One, the Alamo, is now a museum. The other four San Antonio missions are active churches. In California, visitors can journey 600 mi. (1,000 km) along the California Mission Trail to see 21 missions.

Mission San José is known as "the Queen of the Missions."

Mission San José y San Miguel de Aguayo (SAN hoe-ZAY EE SAN mee-GEL DEH ag-WYE-oh) was the largest mission in San Antonio, Texas.

Spanish Influence

The Spanish missions helped shape the United States and changed the lives of Native Americans. Many U.S. cities grew up around the missions. Foods such as oranges and wheat were first grown on mission farms. But as the Spanish brought these changes to North America, Native Americans struggled to defend themselves against poor treatment and deadly diseases. The lives and land they had known for so many years were forever changed by the Spanish missions. ★

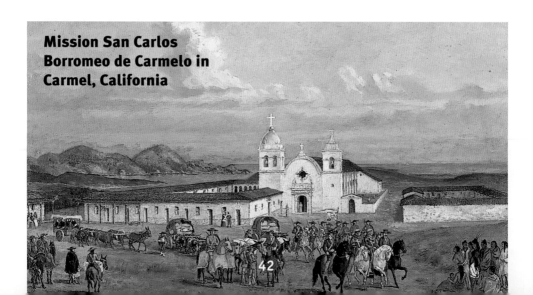

Mission San Carlos Borromeo de Carmelo in Carmel, California

42

True Statistics

First mission founded in the United States:
Mission Nombre de Dios, St. Augustine, Florida

Size of Francisco Vázquez de Coronado's army:
336 soldiers, 800 Mexican Indians, and 5 priests

Number of years the Spanish used the Alamo as a mission: 75

Number of missions started by Father Kino: 29 in both Mexico and the American Southwest

Number of missions founded by Father Serra: 9

Did you find the truth?

F All of the Spanish missions built in what is now the United States are in ruins.

T Native Americans lived at the Spanish missions.

43

Resources

Books

Bial, Raymond. *Missions and Presidios.* New York: Children's Press, 2004.

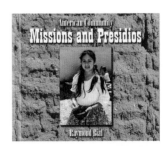

Higgins, Nadia. *Spanish Missions of the Old West.* Vero Beach, FL: Rourke Publishing, 2007.

Kalman, Bobbie, and Greg Nickles. *Spanish Missions.* New York: Crabtree Publishing, 1997.

Leffingwell, Randy. *California Missions and Presidios.* Stillwater, MN: Voyageur Press, 2005.

MacMillan, Dianne M. *Los Angeles Area Missions.* Minneapolis: Lerner Publishing, 2008.

Nelson, Libby, and Kari Cornell. *California Missions Projects and Layouts.* Minneapolis: Lerner Publishing, 2008.

Staeger, Rob. *The Spanish Missions of California.* Broomall, PA: Mason Crest, 2003.

Organizations and Web Sites

California State Parks: The California Missions Trail

www.parks.ca.gov/?page_id=22722

Information about each of California's 21 missions is featured at this site.

Old Spanish Mission of San Antonio

www.oldspanishmissions.org

Take a virtual tour of four of the San Antonio missions.

Spanish Missions: National Hispanic Heritage Month

www.loc.gov/topics/hispanicheritage/missions/

View more pictures of Spanish missions.

Places to Visit

The Alamo

300 Alamo Plaza

San Antonio, Texas 78299

(210) 225-1391

www.thealamo.org

At this historic site, visitors can see one of the best-known Spanish missions.

Historic Mission San Juan Capistrano

Historic Mission San Juan Capistrano

26801 Ortega Highway

San Juan Capistrano, CA 92675

(949) 234-1300

www.missionsjc.com

Visit and explore the ruins of Mission San Juan Capistrano.

Important Words

baptize – to make someone a member of a church through a ceremony in which that person is either dipped in or sprinkled with water

claimed – demanded as one's right

conquistadors (kawn-KEES-tuh-dorz) – Spanish soldiers who conquered Native people in North and South America

continent – one of Earth's seven major areas of land. These are Africa, Antarctica, Asia, Australia, Europe, North America, and South America.

convert – to change someone's beliefs

customs – activities that are practiced a lot

droughts (DROWTS) – long periods without rain

empire – a group of people under one ruler or government

expedition – a journey taken for a specific purpose

presidios (prih-SEE-dee-ohz) – forts that the Spanish built for protection

revolt – an act of rising up and fighting against

Index

Page numbers in **bold** indicate illustrations

47

About the Author

John Perritano is an award-winning journalist and author of many nonfiction books for children. He holds a master's degree in U.S. history from Western Connecticut State University. He is a former senior editor at Scholastic. He has written other True Books, including *The Transcontinental Railroad* and *The Lewis and Clark Expedition*. He lives in Southbury, Connecticut, with three dogs, three cats, and three frogs.